The Videogame Economy

The Videogame Economy

Counter Strike: Global Offensive and its
Collectible Investments

Acknowledgements

I would like to thank my academic and life mentor, Mr. Johnny López-Figueroa, for pushing me to be the best version of myself and aiding me in the process of writing this book and doing research on the subject. Thanks to my family for supporting me, everyone who read my manuscript, and you reading right now. This book is dedicated to my family and my little sister, whose unwavering curiosity gives me the motivation to learn every day.

*Investing isn't about beating others at their game. It's about controlling yourself at your own **game**.*

–Benjamin Graham

Table of Contents

Introduction

In the ever-evolving landscape of digital economies, where Non-Fungible Tokens (NFTs) flaunt a colossal $16 billion USD valuation as of 2022, a subtle yet burgeoning competitor has continued growing in size—videogame economies. Consider the ascent of Kyle Giersdorf, known as Bugha, a 16-year-old professional esports player who clinched victory in the Solo World Cup of Fortnite, earning a staggering $2.7 million USD by playing the game. Similar success stories are etched in the realm of competitive gaming, with Counter-Strike: Global Offensive (CS:GO) standing tall as not merely a form of entertainment but a bona fide competitive sport, boasting an estimated billion-dollar economy valuation and garnering millions of views online.

CS:GO, a multiplayer, first-person competitive shooter meticulously crafted by Valve Corporation, introduced an ingenious method to captivate players—the allure of tradeable microtransaction items known as "skins." These are customizable cosmetic items that alter the appearance of in-game weapons. These skins, acquired through microtransactions, not only elevate the player experience but also create an additional revenue stream for the developers. Each skin, endowed with a unique ID, ensures that no two skins, even if sharing the same name, are identical. Sticker customizations and a "Stat Trak" possibility, which will both be discussed later, add to the uniqueness of a skin. The acquisition of skins unfolds through cases— a thrilling, casino-style experience where players invest a fixed "key" cost to unlock a case and unveil a random skin with varying rarities. The creation of cases is intrinsically linked to the number of active gamers, creating a dynamic market where supply and demand harmonize with the flow of the game's popularity and loyal player base.

The ensuing journey for players involves the exchange of these items on Valve's Steam Community Market for credits, a virtual currency convertible into video games or other skins, creating a self-sustaining economy. Valve further augments this ecosystem with a trading system, fostering a secondary market curated by independent corporations, paving the way for intriguing possibilities—using items as gambling currency, renting coveted items, deploying trading bots, and engaging in market manipulation.

The meteoric rise of CS:GO, fueled by the anticipation surrounding the recently released sequel "CS2," resounding competitive tournaments featuring life-changing cash prizes, and a vibrant community of skin collectors and content creators, has precipitated an unprecedented surge in skin sales. Even with these remarkable dynamics, the game's secondary market never fails to astonish. Skins, in the realm of this market, command prices soaring into thousands of real-world dollars, exemplified by a recent offer of 1.5 million USD for a single knife skin.

The windfall isn't exclusive to players and collectors alone; Valve reaps significant benefits, with monthly earnings scaling up to 54 million USD. The market has burgeoned to a scale where many now categorize it as a collectible, joining the ranks of artworks, NFTs, books, and other items that fetch multiples of their original price. This book embarks on a journey to do what no other has before—unravel the intricacies of the market Valve ingeniously birthed with CS:GO, offering a guide for investors navigating this uncharted territory—a new alternative investment that has proven to yield exponential returns.

This book aims to be the first to explain this novel concept: Why are players flocking to spend thousands of dollars on virtual collectibles? How are investors profiting from this new market created by Valve? How can any reader find opportunity in this emerging and developing sector?

The Virtual Marketplace

Before contextualizing the economic potential of CSGO, its worth considering its roots in microtransactions. The following chapter discusses the growth of cosmetic items in videogames as a new income source for companies, and a new facet of enjoyment for players.

The Evolution of Microtransactions

The Cambridge Dictionary defines a microtransaction as a payment of very small value, especially for a special feature of a product such as a videogame. The gaming subculture has been around since the rise in popularity of video games in the 1980s. As gaming technology advanced, video game companies found new methods to monetize and add value to their content. During the late 2000s, game companies started profiting more with their game via microtransactions. The original purpose of the microtransaction was to enhance the gamer's experience while playing a game, but in some instances, it turned into a way to get players to pay more to succeed. Players would complain about these microtransactions when they became a prominent aspect of online games, since they made some "pay-to-win".

The microtransaction business model originated in 2006 with companies such as Microsoft and Bethesda adding content that would alter the playable character's appearance in-game for a price. This naturally led to controversy, as some users were outraged that they had to pay for content on a videogame that already cost 60 USD, while others were amazed at the new possibility for flexibility in their user experience. In the end, Bethesda was glad as they had the opportunity to have an additional income source from a single game. The microtransaction business model grew in popularity in the sector in 2014, as mobile games such as "Angry Birds" and "Clash of Clans" became house-hold names, and the scheme gave way for free-to-play games to start generating income and provide additional value for the players. Many companies apart from mobile games have adopted this free-to-play model with microtransactions, including CS:GO becoming free on December 6, 2018. Apart from microtransactions adding cosmetic value to the game, the other major selling point companies use is DLC (downloadable content), which gives extra missions or other playable sequences for players at an additional cost.

An example of consumer outrage led by "pay-to-win" microtransactions is when Electronic Arts (EA) released Star Wars Battlefront 2. In the game, it would take hours, to unlock characters like Luke Skywalker, Darth Vader, etc., but players could pay to access these characters. Microtransactions like these made the game pay-to-win. It meant that players who would pay more to gain these characters would have an advantage over those who didn't pay for them. When gamers complained, the company response did not calm people down. EA said that the reason for making it difficult to obtain these characters was to give gamers a sense of accomplishment when they unlocked them. It became one of the most disliked responses on the internet. Microtransactions like the one that EA implemented are the problem with the new monetization technique. However, not all microtransactions are viewed negatively by the gaming subculture, like skins in the CS:GO market. These microtransactions are seen in a more positive light because they aren't a necessary purchase to enjoy the game or progress the story.

Recently, the pandemic allowed video game corporations to sell more, as players had increased consumption time. This otherwise unfortunate event allowed the industry to grow, and it has continued breaking sales records. The Games as a Service model (GaaS) has proven beneficial for users and creators. Companies can remain profitable after their initial release, with the option to have more monetization available indefinitely. For players, the business model allows the games to continually feel interesting and novel because there is a perpetual set of new services that can range in size and type.

In the 2014 Games Developers Conference, Valve's Bronwen Grimes was able to explicate the methods the company used to develop a microtransactions market for CS:GO. They tried mimicking luxury brands, which are notorious for using various psychological tactics to better sell their products. The most important thing they added was a randomized scarcity, since the quality of skins and type is exponentially harder to obtain, the better they are. They instantly found that the time spent using a particular weapon influenced the price of it, hence why an AK-47 skin, which is highly used by player, usually cost more than a PP-Bizon for example, which isn't as popular. This is what essentially drives the demand for skins, and the reason this market can have investment potential in the first place. Users have access to flaunt their hard-to-obtain skins, and since it's a competitive game, eSports competitions, content creators, and influencers (like Neymar, who is a big fan of the game) can also affect the demand exponentially, as they can be market movers and promote certain weapon "loadouts" to their fans.

The Steam Community Market

This chapter introduces the Steam Community Market, the official marketplace for all transactions within the Counter: Strike Community. It also discusses the different content creators and outside developments that have affected the growth and stability of the market.

The Official Skin Market of CS:GO

CS:GO is a first-person shooter game where each team needs to win a specific number of rounds to win the game. In each round, any side of team will receive a score or round win. Players are divided into two teams of Terrorist and Counter-Terrorist with different set objectives. For the Terrorist team, their objective is to successfully plant and detonate the bomb or to eliminate all the counter-terrorist team. For the Counter-Terrorist team, their objective is to prevent the Terrorist team from detonating the bomb or eliminate all the Terrorist team. In an official CS:GO competitive or tournament match, the first team reaching 16 rounds win out of 30 rounds will be the winner, and in case of a draw after 30 rounds, an overtime will be played with maximum 6 rounds. CS:GO has competitive matchmaking, matching players equally based on their skill group, adding to the intensity of the matches. Being matched to a higher skill group is a badge of honor, giving more incentive for players to learn the game and practice their tactics. In each round, both teams may have equal possibility to win. Even though in the previous round terrorist team won, counter-terrorist team will still have possibility to win the next round or vice versa. The combination of the two-aspect result can be seen in the popularity of the CS:GO. Since their release on the August 21, 2012, according to SteamSpy, CS:GO has sold and been downloaded over 70 million times in total, with high user ratings and averages more than 700,000 monthly active players. CS:GO was also awarded as "Best eSports Game of The Year" on The Game Awards 2015 and has been nominated for "Best Esports Game" at the 2017, 2019, 2020, 2021, and 2022 The Game Awards, among others.

The Steam Marketplace allows users to purchase skins from other players in a format similar to an auction or the stock market, instead of solely selling them themselves. Collectors, players, and investors impact each other by their actions in the digital market. Valve controls the supply by creating new "cases" with "operations" and in-game "drops." The unique system that adds value to a skin is by the probability distribution of obtaining a certain skin, which is skewed by quality. The exact "float", meaning the % of quality of an item, is also randomized. After opening a case, a player can list it on the open market or trade it for another one with any player. Skins can vary in pricing dramatically, with the lowest possible price being 0.03 USD, and the most expensive being 2,200 USD on the Steam Community Market. The entire market is estimated to have a market capitalization of over a billion dollars. The most relevant determinant in the valuation of a skin is whether it is a gun or not since knives and gloves are more challenging to obtain and more sought out by the community because they are seen more in-game.

Cases are items that are dropped occasionally after a match concludes in the videogame, and it grants the opener an item inside. There are multiple iterations of cases. The price of the case is determined by the market's desire of the skins inside the case through buy/sell orders users initiate. They are opened with keys, which have a current flat cost of $2.50 and can only be used to open a case a single time. Skins have different qualities, which determine their rarity. The rarity of an item is determined by its color. In CS:GO, there are six tiers of rarity. The lowest tier is Consumer Grade, which is indicated by a light blue text, followed by Industrial Grade, a navy-blue text. These two colors are exclusively only available through in-game drops and are the most common. Mil-Spec Grade (dark blue), Restricted (purple),

Classified (pink) and Covert (red) weapons are available through case-opening. Covert is currently the highest rarity of weapons available in CS:GO.

These skins have different assigned wear values, ranging from factory new to battle scarred. These rankings are Factory New (0.00-0.07), Minimal Wear (0.07-0.15), Field-Tested (0.15-0.37), Well-Worn (0.37-0.44) or Battle- Scarred (0.44-1). The closer an item is in wear value to 0, the closer it is to Factory New. StatTrak items are rarer and can apply to any wear value. They show the gamer how many kills they got in- game with the weapon. This rarity usually adds an exponential add to the skin's value, as it gives a new layer of possibility for players to flaunt their in-game skil as well. There is no official way to sell a skin for real-world cash since sales on the Steam Community Market give Steam Store Credit. Real-World money is obviously valued more than Steam Credit; hence the reason why third-party sites sell skins for a cheaper price relative to the Steam Community Market. CS:GO Trading has also opened an avenue for gamers to use skins in third-party betting sites as a currency, which will be discussed further on in Chapter five.

CS:GO skins are considered a speculative asset class that consumers buy primarily in the expectation of future prices, not necessarily according to their individual preferences. It is one of the first of many markets that start purely as consumer goods but are financialized because of the high transaction speeds and low marginal costs, being a completely virtual market with no reliance on real-world transactions. There is also a high similarity between the speculative peculiarities found in CS:GO skins and cryptocurrencies, leading to the belief that they work similarly in their price movements. This leads to some successful investors diverting some of their games into skins. In the digital age, content creators wield significant influence, and in the world of Counter-Strike: Global Offensive (CS:GO), they have emerged as pivotal figures shaping the dynamics of the skin economy. This influence, often likened to the impact of financial pundits like Jim Cramer in the stock market, has transformed CS:GO into a realm where publicized predictions and content can sway pricing and market trends.

The Rise of Content Creators in the CS:GO Market

In the absence of official recognition as an investment vehicle by governments, the CS:GO market operates with near-zero regulation, paving the way for influencers to play a central role in its growth. Much like traditional financial markets, these content creators can influence sentiment, trigger speculative trading, and even spark meme-driven phenomena within the community. The impact of content creators on pricing is palpable. Just as in the stock market where public figures can move markets with their statements, CS:GO influencers, armed with massive followings, can significantly affect the pricing of in-game items. The lack of regulation, while fostering creativity and individual freedom, also opens the door to pump-and-dump schemes and investment decisions guided by memes and sub-cultural trends. An illustrative case in point is the P250 Sand Dune, which became a meme due to its high volume and seemingly unremarkable appearance. This created a unique market dynamic, leading to occasional spikes in its price as a result of online challenges, trading trends, and professional-player recommendations within the gaming community. Another example is the quest for high-float items, partially because of their meme value. The influence of content creators extends to shaping the perception of items, creating a symbiotic relationship where market trends and memes intertwine to form the market value of items.

A subset of CS:GO investors double as content creators, showcasing their investment strategies, unboxings, and trade-up contracts on platforms like YouTube. TDM Heyzeus stands out as one of the most prominent CS:GO content creators, amassing over 150 million views with videos that delve into various facets of the skin economy. His content not only educates viewers but also indirectly promotes certain cases by featuring them in unboxings, thus driving demand. He also features other players' collections, adding to the popularity (or notoriety) of certain skins. TDM Heyzeus's influence is particularly noteworthy. With a vast viewership, his videos on case unboxings and trade-up contracts create a ripple effect in the market. Case unboxings, a popular genre in CS:GO content creation, elevate the desirability of specific cases and the skins they contain. This heightened demand, fueled by the influencer's endorsement, can lead to increased market activity, with players eager to replicate the experiences showcased in these videos. Often, content creators compete for owning the lowest-float items available, adding to the value of low-float Factory New skins. Trade-up contract videos, a form of in-game gambling where players trade lower-tier items for a chance at a higher-tier item, serve both as entertainment/ educational content for potential investors and enthusiasts. Heyzeus's engagement with this game mechanic not only informs his audience but also contributes to market demand for items involved in these contracts. Investors, seeking advice and insights from influencers, may be swayed by their recommendations, affecting the market's supply and demand dynamics.

While content creators bring unprecedented attention and demand to the CS:GO market, their influence also introduces challenges. The potential for pump-and-dump schemes, where creators can inadvertently or intentionally manipulate markets, underscores the need for responsible content creation. Investors, especially those new to the market, should approach recommendations with a discerning eye, understanding the dual nature of content creators as both educators and market influencers, who are almost always invested in the market themselves. The symbiotic relationship between content creators and the CS:GO market showcases the transformative power of digital influencers. The recognized case study of TDM Heyzeus exemplifies how content creators, through their engaging and informative content, can shape market trends, influence pricing, and contribute to the evolving narrative of the CS:GO skin economy. As this relationship continues to evolve, market participants must navigate the opportunities and challenges presented by this dynamic intersection of gaming, content creation, and virtual economies.

Driving Market Forces

China's emergence as a global economic powerhouse has not only reshaped traditional financial markets but also exerted a profound influence on the digital landscapes, including the Counter-Strike: Global Offensive (CS:GO) market. This influence manifests in various facets, ranging from the player base and esports ecosystem to the dynamics of skin trading and investments. China's vast population and its burgeoning interest in esports have significantly contributed to the expansion of the CS:GO player base. The influx of Chinese players into the CS:GO community has not only diversified the gaming landscape but also intensified the competition at both casual and professional levels. This surge in players has not only elevated the skill levels within the game but has also led to an increase in demand for in-game items, especially rare skins.

In the esports realm, China's influence is even more pronounced. The country has become a major hub for CS:GO tournaments, attracting top-tier teams and massive viewership. Tournaments like Perfect World Masters and CS:GO Asia Championships with life-changing prize pools have become staples in the competitive scene, providing a platform for players and teams to showcase their skills. This heightened visibility contributes to the market dynamics as popular players and teams gain increased recognition, impacting the desirability and value of associated skins.

China's regulatory environment plays a crucial role in shaping the CS:GO market. The Chinese government has implemented measures to regulate the gaming industry, including age restrictions and content guidelines. These regulatory actions can influence the market by affecting the number of active players, particularly younger demographics who might be drawn to skin trading. Furthermore, changes in regulations can impact the accessibility and visibility of CS:GO in China, subsequently influencing the demand for in-game items. Moreover, China's broader economic policies and geopolitical developments can have ripple effects on the CS:GO market. Trade tensions or economic shifts can influence currency exchange rates, potentially impacting the value of virtual items. Investors and traders in the CS:GO market must stay attuned to these external factors to make informed decisions.

In parallel to China's influence, the rise of cryptocurrency has introduced a transformative force in the CS:GO market. Cryptocurrencies, such as Bitcoin and Ethereum, have become alternative means of transaction within the gaming community, including the buying and selling of CS:GO skins. The integration of cryptocurrencies has brought about both opportunities and challenges for market participants. Cryptocurrencies offer a decentralized and borderless means of value exchange. In the context of the CS:GO market, this feature is particularly advantageous. Traders and investors from different parts of the world can seamlessly engage in transactions without the traditional constraints associated with fiat currencies. Cryptocurrencies act as a universal medium of exchange, fostering a global marketplace for CS:GO skins. The introduction of cryptocurrencies has injected a new layer of liquidity into the CS:GO market. Traditionally, users would conduct transactions through the Steam Community Market using Steam Balance, meaning profits were complicated to turn into tangible fiat currency. The integration of cryptocurrencies enables faster and more fluid transactions. This increased liquidity has facilitated speculative trading, with market participants capitalizing on price fluctuations to maximize profits. However, this liquidity also introduces an element of volatility. Cryptocurrency prices can be highly volatile, and their influence on CS:GO skin values is not immune to sudden market shifts. Traders must navigate this dynamic landscape with a keen awareness of cryptocurrency market trends and their potential impact on the CS:GO market.

While cryptocurrencies bring novel opportunities, they also pose challenges and security concerns. The decentralized nature of cryptocurrencies means that transactions are irreversible and anonymous, amplifying the risks associated with fraud and scams. The CS:GO market, already susceptible to illicit activities, must grapple with the potential misuse of cryptocurrencies for fraudulent purposes. Furthermore, regulatory uncertainties surrounding cryptocurrencies introduce an additional layer of complexity, especially for tax purposes. The lack of a standardized regulatory framework leaves room for ambiguity, and market participants must navigate this terrain cautiously. Government interventions and regulatory developments in the cryptocurrency space can reverberate into the CS:GO market, impacting transaction practices and user behaviors. Still, crypto has become a better alternative than using the Steam Community Market or PayPal to trade.

Beyond transactions, the marriage of CS:GO skins and cryptocurrencies has inspired other companies to venture into the realm of Blockchain technology. Some platforms are exploring the use of Blockchain to enhance the authenticity and traceability of virtual items. Blockchain's immutable ledger ensures transparency, reducing the risk of counterfeit or fraudulent transactions. Although Valve did not directly motivate this, CS:GO's economy has inspired others to integrate similar and more evolved systems within their game's economies. This integration aligns with the broader trend of incorporating Blockchain in gaming to enhance security and user confidence. Both China's influence and the integration of cryptocurrency have emerged as transformative forces in the Counter-Strike: Global Offensive market. China's expansive player base, esports dominance, and regulatory dynamics shape the market's landscape. Simultaneously, cryptocurrencies offer a decentralized means of transaction, fostering global liquidity and presenting new opportunities for traders and investors. Navigating these influences requires a nuanced understanding of regional dynamics, regulatory landscapes, and the evolving intersection of virtual economies with global financial trends. Market participants must adapt to the ever-changing dynamics, leveraging opportunities while mitigating risks in this intricate fusion of gaming, economics, and technology. These changes serve as a foresight into implementations of NFT technology and the increased globalization/digitalization of the economy. In the next chapter, we will explore how NFTs square up to the CS:GO Market.

The Collectibles Market

This chapter will discuss the Non-Fungibles Token (NFT) market, as well as collectibles as a whole, showing a brief history of it. With this information, we can discuss how it pertains and relates to CS:GO and establish similarities between the markets.

The NFT Market

Non-Fungible Tokens (NFTs) are digital titles to real or virtual property that are stored in a cryptocurrency blockchain. NFT's activities rely on many factors such as the Blockchain and the use of Smart Contracts. The Blockchain uses the proof of work algorithm to distribute data in a decentralized network. Using cryptography, the Blockchain protects data records which can be used for NFTs, currencies ,and other items. It solves the problem of having a network filled with untrusted participants, since it functions as a third-party for otherwise high-risk transactions. The Blockchain hosts smart contracts, which are used to produce NFTs. These contracts work as a method to accelerate, verify, and complete digital negotiations. They enable unknown parties to complete transactions in a decentralized manner, hence why it is used for NFT minting and exchanges. They work as an equalizing factor since there is completely transparency to the execution of all transactions and all sides have equal parameters. This democratic economy has given sway to a new array of economic activities.

This digital revolution has affected various industries such as: the art market, collectibles, gaming, luxury goods, fashion, music, entertainment, and real estate. According to author Mekacher and others in *Heterogeneous rarity patterns drive price dynamics in NFT collections*, the market has grown more than 61,000% throughout 2021, and it was named the Collins Dictionary word of the year. They are often sold as a collection with similar visual aspects or code, normally as a generative art form. NFTs are frequently made using a predetermined algorithm, which uses an element of chance to generate the different iterations of the tokens. One of the most famous collections are CryptoPunks, a collection of pixelated human faces and the Bored Ape Yacht Club, which consists of 10,000 cartoon apes. Their market capitalizations sat around 2.5B USD and 3.8B USD respectively as of March 2022, although they have since been reduced. Successful investors in this market have diversified their portfolio into various industries, such as CS:GO assets. In the study previously mentioned, they discovered that a higher rarity led to less sales of an NFT, but the price sold rose exponentially the rarer the attributes the art had were. At the same time, rarer items overall had a less likelihood to produce negative returns for prospective investors. This can be related to how other collectibles function in terms of their financial value.

NFTs have great potential for being applied to the gaming industry because the reward of being able to sell gaming items as a digital good can attract a wide array of investors to participate in the videogame. NFTs also validate the ownership of of gaming items to the players, providing added value and connection to the gameplay in the process since items are exclusive to the user. Both players and developers benefit from the secondary NFT market, creating a symbiotic relationship.

NFTs, as mentioned earlier, leverage Blockchain technology and Smart Contracts to establish ownership and facilitate secure transactions. In contrast, CS:GO's skin market operates within the confines of the game's ecosystem, utilizing a centralized infrastructure managed by Valve Corporation. Despite this technological disparity, both NFTs and CS:GO skins hinge on the concept of rarity and uniqueness to confer value. In CS:GO, players covet rare and aesthetically pleasing weapon skins, often attributing prestige to those with limited availability. This parallels the scarcity-driven value proposition in the NFT space, where rarity and exclusivity contribute significantly to an asset's perceived worth, which is necessary since it has no intrinsic value or future cash flow.

A significant divergence lies in the decentralization aspect. NFTs, owing to their blockchain foundation, operate in a decentralized and tamper-proof environment, promoting transparency and security. On the contrary, the CS:GO skin market relies on Valve's centralized servers, which introduces an additional layer of control and potential concerns related to governance and oversight. Furthermore, all transactions are recorded by Valve and shown on the Steam Community Market, with a lesser degree of scrutiny and transparency. This simultaneously gives the market more internal security and less external since the investors depend completely on Valve's actions without any vote.

The cultural impact of both NFTs and CS:GO skins extends beyond their respective niches. NFTs have ignited conversations about the digitization of art, environmental concerns related to blockchain networks, and the democratization of ownership. Similarly, the CS:GO skin market has prompted ethical discussions, particularly in relation to underage gambling, as skins can be traded for real-world currency on third-party platforms. These considerations highlight the importance of responsible management in digital markets and the need to address ethical challenges arising from these innovative trends, which will only continue to increase.

Moreover, the market dynamics and investment principles share common ground. Just as NFTs exhibit varying levels of rarity, influencing their market values, CS:GO skins follow a similar pattern. Scarcer skins in the game's ecosystem command higher prices, creating an economic model that echoes the principles of NFT valuation. This convergence in market behavior emphasizes the broader shifts in digital economies, where the perceived value of virtual assets is increasingly determined by factors such as scarcity, uniqueness, and community demand.

In the context of gaming, both NFTs and CS:GO skins redefine the relationship between players and their virtual possessions. NFTs introduce a novel layer of ownership validation and value enhancement, extending the gaming experience beyond the virtual realm. Similarly, CS:GO players often form strong attachments to their rare skins, viewing them as personal symbols of achievement and status within the gaming community. As these trends continue to evolve, the intersections and distinctions between the NFT trend and the CS:GO skin market offer valuable insights into the multifaceted nature of digital ownership, market dynamics, and the ongoing transformation of various sectors within the digital landscape.

A History of Collectibles Investing

Collectible investments can be any unique object that can increase in market value: from art to alcohol and sports memorabilia. They can have significant appreciation because of their limited quantity and nostalgic factor. In particular periods, these investments have outperformed the stock and bond markets. The primary concern with investing in this category is the difficulty of predicting how factors of rarity, condition, provenance, and market demand will affect long-term value appreciation, if any. These issues are coupled with the low liquidity of the items. One factor that increases the risk factor of these investments is the high maintenance costs. The possibility of counterfeits and forgery of items also increases the risk profile. Investing solely in collectibles poses the investor with a much higher risk compared to traditional investment tools. To successfully benefit from these investments, it is valuable to have due diligence and research the sector properly. Creating a diversified portfolio with more traditional investment tools can reduce risk exposure. Especially in this market, it is valuable to have patience and wait for the right time, due to the long-term nature of these investments, which don't offer predictable selling opportunities. It is also beneficial to network with experts in the field to better understand the market, and more easily find worthy items. All collectible investments are subject to applicable taxes including but not limited to capital and estate taxes.

Most items worth more currently than when they were produced are considered collectibles: there are countless sub-categories in this asset class. Collectibles are a type of alternative asset, alongside others such as cryptocurrency and NFTs, private equity, commodities, real estate, and others. According to Business Insider, collectibles have had the potential to outperform the stock market, such as stamps in the GB250 Index, which tracks Great Britain's top 250 stamps, growing more than 13 percent per annum since 1991. These investments can add to the diversification of a portfolio, which is the best risk management strategy.

This asset class is not closely correlated to the stock market, meaning it does not necessarily fluctuate in value due to the same circumstances as traditional investment vehicles, creating a different time horizon for selling. It has the potential for a massive return on investment. For example, some of the original Star Wars merchandise for the first movie has had an ROI of up to 155,000 percent according to Self, Inc. The portability of some collectibles allows for easier transportation and a greater level of control. Collectibles also have the holistic enjoyment factor, which can subjectively be more valuable than investing in the stock market or bonds. The downside of collectible investments is that they have no intrinsic value. Their value is dependent on their condition and public perception; there is always the risk of fraudulent activity as well.

Most money invested in the portfolio of a high net-worth individual is traditional, as the industry has a culture and long-held beliefs that lead to a natural unwillingness to take on new ideas, especially ones with such a different valuation approach. According to According to financial author Stephen Satchell in the book *Collectible investments for the high-net-worth investor,* the process for building a portfolio can be broken down into five steps: gathering information from the client, creating an investor profile, building an asset universe, constructing the portfolio, and reviewing it with the client. In the case of CS:GO, this process is done exclusively by the investor, as finding proper consulting is near-impossible. Satchell states that collectible investing has many benefits apart from a return, such as enjoying the benefits of status and having the item itself. This social aspect is not traditionally considered in a portfolio, even when it might be a relevant factor in the decision process of a potential investor. This concept of having "bragging rights" is a pertinent factor in purchasing a novel collectible. These high net-worth investors usually have a higher risk profile and also enjoy the inherent process of building a collection, which cannot be valued by a traditional asset manager. A problem that arises from this is that the collector may overvalue their items or get overexposed to a certain facet of the market, as emotional decisions are much more common in this asset class.

Collectibles have some risks that are valuable to consider. Inherently, they are speculative assets and provide no dividend income, unlike more traditional assets, like bonds and value stocks. They have also underperformed the stock market in some circumstances. They can be ineffective as a liquid market hedge, as most collectibles are considered highly illiquid, depending on their categorical value, which can vary wildly. They are subject to the cultural mode and other contemporary factors that might affect their long-term investment potential. Most high-value collectibles are also subject to high maintenance costs, risks of natural disasters, and other circumstances affecting the value of an item negatively; these apply to a much lesser extent to traditional investments, such as owning equity in corporations. Collecting is an interesting phenomenon since it is not purely considered a consumption activity, but also not solely an investment. According to Professor James Kleine and others in *Rich men's hobby or question of personality: who considers collectibles as alternative investment?*, most investor collectors have attained a higher education, high income, and available financial assets. They generally have a broader range of interests and a higher risk profile, so they find collecting rewarding not only from an economic perspective but also for the purpose of owning a novel item.

In comprehensive research done by professors Benjamin J. Burton and Joyce P. Jacobsen in *Measuring Returns on Investments in collectibles*, almost no study analyzed showed a negative nominal rate of return, showing the potential value in holding collectibles as an alternative investment. The indexes showed annual returns in the range of 11 to 14 percent over periods of 13 to 21 years, a higher average than the S&P 500. It is considered that collectibles embody a much higher risk than any other financial asset. The most relevant factor that affects most of the return in collectible investing is the requirement of reliable storage space/special handling, as well as using market makers like auction houses and third-party dealers. Collectibles could serve as a hedge to other investment vehicles like the stock market, as some studies have found that they incur a negative correlation with returns on financial assets, although a consensus by researchers has not been reached.

For example, various authors suggested in 1995 on *Stamp Returns and Economic Factors*, based on the 1947-1988 period, that stamps have opposite sensitivities to stocks concerning inflation and other factors, meaning they could be a potential hedge. Collectible mutual funds have yet to come to fruition, limiting the expansion of the asset class into a broader financial market. The closest the industry has come to mutual funds has been fractional investment platforms such as Otis and Masterworks, with some focusing on a specific asset class and others selling fractional shares of any type of collectible investment. Masterworks has had items with an annualized net return of 788.9%, yet most of these investments still pale in comparison to institutional investments. The only historical instance of major institutional investing in collectibles has been with the British Rail pension fund that invested a significant amount (around 3% of their holdings at the time) into the art market with Sotheby's. The decision resulted in a suboptimal return; by the time they liquidated their holdings, they had a 13.8 percent per annum return while British stocks averaged 21.5 percent.

Some studies theorize that alternate investments in collectibles are positively correlated with the financial asset markets since stock investors become richer due to returns and spend part of their gains on collectibles such as art. The biggest issue in the collectible industry overall is the frequently exhibited boom-bust patterns, which are exacerbated by the possibility of regional points of sale majorly differing in price, causing bargains and over-pricing simultaneously. Fortunately, the internet and more efficiency in the dissemination of information have lowered this issue, establishing more stable collectible markets and more reliable sources of information. This is precisely what has been seen in the CSGO market, as influencers solidify positions in certain cases and skins, while collectively discarding others.

The dynamics of the collectibles market draw intriguing comparisons to the recently-established CS:GO skin market, both of which revolve around unique, and often nostalgic, items. In the realm of collectibles, investments span a wide array of categories, such as art, sports memorabilia, and alcohol, emphasizing the diversity within this alternative asset class. Similarly, in CS:GO, players seek unique and visually appealing weapon skins, each holding its own nostalgic and aesthetic significance.

A key parallel lies in the challenge of predicting factors influencing value. In the collectibles market, rarity, condition, provenance, and market demand are pivotal, mirroring the importance of these elements in the CS:GO skin market. Limited edition skins, those with pristine wear-values, and those with historical significance often command higher values, creating a market where predicting these factors can be as challenging as it is essential.

The illiquidity of extremely rare items in both collectibles and CS:GO skins introduces a shared element of risk. The risk factors associated with maintenance costs and the potential for counterfeits also resonate with the CS:GO skin market, where third-party trading platforms introduce additional complexities and costs, albeit much lower than their physical counterparts. Furthermore, the social and status aspects of collectibles investing find a counterpart in the CS:GO community. Similar to traditional collectibles, in the CS:GO skin market, the rarity and exclusivity of certain skins contribute to a player's status within the gaming community, solidifying its market value and prestige.

The notion that collectibles can outperform the stock market echoes the dynamic seen in the CS:GO skin market, where certain rare skins can yield substantial returns. However, both markets are not without their risks; the aforementioned issues of illiquidity and vulnerability to market fluctuations are challenges that investors and players face. The role of studies and analyses in the collectibles market, predicting returns and correlations, bears resemblance to the informal research and analysis undertaken by CS:GO players and enthusiasts to assess the value and potential profitability of in-game skins. Additionally, the boom-bust patterns find a parallel in the history of the CS:GO skin market, which has witnessed fluctuations in skin prices driven by similar factors.

Comparing the Stock Market and CS:GO Returns

Examining the supremely rare Katowice 2014 sticker prices in CS:GO offers a microcosm of the virtual economy's dynamics. The initial prices of these stickers, commemorating the 2014 CS:GO tournament in Katowice, Poland (one of the first CS:GO tournaments in history), experienced exponential growth over the years. For instance, a Titan Katowice 2014 hologram sticker, initially priced at a few dollars, surged to thousands in subsequent years. This phenomenal appreciation mirrors the growth potential seen in certain stocks within the traditional market. Conversely, scrutinizing the financial figures of the S&P 500 index provides a macroscopic view of stock market dynamics. Over the past decade, the S&P 500 has witnessed substantial growth. For instance, from 2011 to 2021, the S&P 500's compound annual growth rate (CAGR) was approximately 13.6%. This financial metric reflects the consistent upward trajectory of leading stocks, akin to the appreciation of high-demand CS:GO stickers. A Katowice 2014 Legends Capsule currently sells for around 10,000 USD (before the market cut and taxes) and only cost 25 cents on release on March 6, 2014. This means a staggering 194% annualized ROI over an investment length of a bit less than a decade. Compare this to buying a single share of Amazon stock the same day, sitting at 18.70 a share. Even being one of the best performing tech stocks of all time, it would still only produce a 68% annualized return. This insane number somehow feels small to the possible return of the historically best CS:GO investments.

The concept of scarcity, pivotal in both realms, is exemplified by the AWP Dragon Lore skin in CS:GO. Initially priced around a few hundred dollars, this rare skin skyrocketed in value. In 2018, a Factory New AWP Dragon Lore was sold for a staggering $61,052, showcasing the extreme scarcity premium attached to certain virtual items. In the stock market, similarly rare assets, such as Berkshire Hathaway's Class A shares priced over $400,000 each, highlight the market's acknowledgment of scarcity, since they have much more voting rights compared to Class B.

Market dynamics in both spheres respond to external stimuli, reflected in specific financial events. In the stock market, Tesla, a prominent and volatile stock, witnessed astronomical growth. In 2010, Tesla's stock traded at around $19 per share, and by 2021, it reached over $600 per share, demonstrating the impact of corporate events and market sentiment, and even sensationalism with memes, since Elon Musk, CEO of Tesla, frequently promoted them. Likewise, CS:GO skin prices surged during major tournaments, reminiscent of stock rallies in response to corporate developments. Risk and volatility, quantifiable through financial metrics, validate the challenges and opportunities in both markets. The volatility index (VIX) in the stock market, often referred to as the "fear index," surged during periods of uncertainty. In CS:GO, the famous and renowned Doppler phase possiblity in knives exemplifies virtual volatility, with prices fluctuating significantly based on aesthetic preferences and market trends.

Investor behavior and sentiment, quantifiable through metrics like trading volumes and sentiment indexes, wield substantial influence. In the stock market, the surge in trading volumes for meme stocks like GameStop during the Reddit-fueled frenzy reflects the power of collective investor sentiment and comedic value. Similarly, the popularity of CS:GO skins associated with renowned players, reflected in trading volumes and market trends, emphasizes the sway of community sentiment. Regulation and oversight, paramount in traditional markets, contrast with the less-regulated nature of the CS:GO skin market. The lack of comprehensive regulatory frameworks in the virtual realm exposes investors to potential risks, distinguishing it from the robust oversight in traditional financial markets.

The power of community and social influence, observable through metrics like online discussions and social media trends, manifests in both markets. In the stock market, the influence of social media platforms on stock prices, exemplified by the GameStop saga, echoes the sway of online discussions on CS:GO skin values. The impact of influential streamers and gaming personalities in promoting specific skins mirrors the effect of celebrity endorsements on stock prices. In essence, the financial figures associated with the growth of CS:GO stickers and the S&P 500 illuminate the converging and diverging trajectories of these asset classes. From the extraordinary appreciation of specific stickers to the robust growth of benchmark indexes, participants in these markets navigate complex landscapes where financial metrics serve as navigational tools in the pursuit of growth and opportunity.

Investing in CS:GO

This chapter aims to develop the different strategies utilized by investors in the market to grow their portfolio on a smaller and larger scale. Some use these methods to be able to purchase more games and enrich their hobbies; some have created a career from the videogame economy.

Retail Arbitrage

In the intricate realm of the CS:GO skin market, a strategic approach known as retail arbitrage has emerged as a potential avenue for users to grow their Steam Wallet Balance. The Steam Community Market, resembling an auction or the stock market, allows users to engage in bidding on items, aiming to secure them at a favorable price. At the same time, sellers compete to offer the lowest price. While Steam does levy a 15% cut, savvy traders identify items with relative liquidity and a spread exceeding the 15%, positioning them as prime candidates for profitable trading.

The mechanics of retail arbitrage on the Steam Community Market are akin to a financial marketplace. Users can strategically bid on items, leveraging the market's dynamics to acquire assets at lower costs. Despite the 15% deduction by Steam, items with sufficient liquidity and a healthy spread offer traders an opportunity to swiftly grow their Steam Wallet Balance, similar to day/swing traders in the market or resellers of physical collectible goods. The agility of this method lies in the ability to promptly relist and sell acquired items, fostering a cycle of growth for astute traders. However, the caveat lies in the limitations of utilizing a Steam Wallet Balance. Purchases are confined to other skins and video games within the Steam ecosystem, restricting opportunities for real investors seeking cash returns unless they opt to sell acquired items on third-party websites, complicating the "cash-out" process.

Expanding beyond the Steam Community Market, users can employ a similar tactic in third-party CS:GO exchanges, contingent on the percentage cut these platforms take per sale. For higher-valued items, a nuanced form of arbitrage trading emerges, particularly with skins adorned with rare stickers. The valuation of such skins hinges on intricate factors, including sticker placement, skin-sticker synergy, and other nuanced elements. This complexity can translate into increased profitability, given that many players lack the expertise to accurately appraise the value of stickers on a skin. However, the execution of this strategy demands a level of expertise and experience, as evaluating the true worth of a sticker-laden item often requires trial and error.

Case Investing

In the multifaceted universe of Counter-Strike: Global Offensive (CS:GO), where virtual skins have evolved into a form of digital currency, a unique avenue for investment has emerged—case investing. Unlike traditional financial markets, CS:GO introduces an unconventional concept where virtual cases, akin to mystery boxes, serve as the entry point for potential financial gains. At its core, case investing revolves around the acquisition, holding, and eventual resale of virtual cases within the CS:GO ecosystem. These cases, which players obtain through in-game drops or purchases, contain a variety of skins, each with its own rarity and market value. The allure of case investing lies in the unpredictability of the items within, similar to the excitement of opening a physical mystery box or a gift.

The CS:GO market dynamics make case investing a distinctive venture. Cases are created based on the number of active players, introducing an element of scarcity tied directly to the game's popularity. This scarcity factor, combined with the randomized nature of item drops within cases, sets the stage for a unique investment landscape. As cases become scarcer due to fluctuations in player engagement, their market value can experience oscillations, offering shrewd investors opportunities for strategic entry and exit points. The process begins with the acquisition of cases, which can be obtained through in-game drops, purchased from the Steam Community Market, 3rd party sites, or through trades. Once in possession of these virtual containers, investors play the waiting game, allowing the scarcity and demand factors to influence the market value of the cases over time.

The potential returns from case investing are not solely reliant on the contents of the cases but are also influenced by broader market trends and the flow of the CS:GO player base. The announcement of major tournaments, updates, or the release of new cases often triggers spikes in player engagement, directly impacting the demand for cases and, consequently, their market value. However, navigating the realm of case investing requires a keen understanding of market trends, player behaviors, and the broader CS:GO ecosystem. Successful investors monitor the case prices frequently, capitalize on events that stimulate player interest, and strategically time their investments to maximize returns. Moreover, case investing extends beyond individual player strategies, forming an integral part of the broader CS:GO market landscape. The interplay between case investors and other market participants creates a dynamic environment where supply, demand, and scarcity intertwine, shaping the overall market sentiment.

While case investing introduces an element of unpredictability and risk, it underscores the dynamic nature of the CS:GO economy. While some are driven by the thrill of unboxing virtual "holy grails" and others are pursuing exponential investment gains, all participants in the case investing arena contribute to the vibrant and evolving ecosystem that defines CS:GO's unique position at the intersection of gaming and alternative investment.

Trading

As with any other economy, CS:GO has a burgeoning trading community. Through Discord messaging groups, Reddit, and the Steam Community forums, many players choose to interchange their skins with others to make a profit or obtain an item they truly desire. This has led to many "challenges" being promoted on the internet, such as some players trying to trade their way from the previously mentioned P2500 "Sand Dune" to an AWP "Dragon Lore", making thousands in the process.

Investors looking to make a profit from trading must have a comprehensive understanding of market dynamics, since there are many ways to value an item that can affect possible exit strategies. Before an update made by Valve, users were able to trade items for the keys used in case openings. This made it effectively a fiat currency within the economy, making an item's value clearer. Now, without this mediator of trades, and especially with expensive stickers, StatTrak valuations varying among items, and other new indicators of value, it's best to do significant research before trading to make a profit.

Tools are available for the wary investor. Search engine extensions allow users to view an item's estimated price on the market within an instant to make better decisions. Often, the most common method to make a profit is to trade an expensive item for many lower-cost items and charging a fee for it. Gergely Szabo, a known trader in the community, effectively made a living only trading skins. To do this, it is important to have a solid principal amount to garner significant returns, since trading most of the time does not result in a significant profit. Also, it is very useful to have references from other traders and a solid reputation to receive more offers. An important note is that the Steam Website does not allow an item to be traded for one week after a purchase or trade, leaving the potential to make significant gains in a short span of time impossible. With this in mind, trading is still a valuable alternative to making money in the CS:GO Market. It can be mixed with other tactics, such as case investing, to secure a more effective exit strategy and return on investment.

Operations and other Dynamics

The Counter-Strike: Global Offensive (CS:GO) skin market is a virtual economy that pulsates with life, and two key influencers, the Steam Summer Sale, and in-game operations, cast a considerable shadow over its pricing dynamics. Understanding the nuances of these events provides insight into the opportunities that define the CS:GO skin market. The annual Steam Summer Sale is more than just an opportunity for gamers to snag discounted titles; it's a tidal wave that sweeps through the CS:GO skin market, leaving in its wake ripples of activity and shifting market dynamics. The allure of reduced prices prompts a surge in user engagement as players flood the Steam Community Market, sparking a flurry of buying and selling. During the sale, players seek to expand their game collections and sell skins. Investors can take advantage of lower prices or engage in speculative trading. The heightened activity often leads to increased demand for specific liquid skins, particularly those with ubiquitous designs or features. Investors keen on capitalizing on these market movements closely monitor trends, identifying potential investment opportunities as prices fluctuate during and after the Summer Sale. The cyclical nature of this event creates windows of opportunity for consistent strategic trading. The Steam Summer Sale, in essence, serves as a catalyst for short-term market dynamics, where the influx of users drives demand and influences skin prices.

In-game operations introduced by Valve inject dynamism into the CS:GO experience and have a profound impact on the skin market. These operations, marked by the introduction of new maps, game modes, and exclusive cosmetic items, captivate the player base, leading to shifts in market sentiment and pricing. One of the key elements of operations is the introduction of operation-exclusive skins. These limited-time offerings become coveted items as players strive to acquire these unique designs, and more start playing the game. The scarcity factor, amplified by the limited duration of the operation, contributes to the potential appreciation of these skins over time. Investors recognizing the value of exclusivity strategically enter the market during the operation, anticipating future value growth as these items become rarer. Esports tournaments often coincide with in-game operations, creating a synergetic effect. Skins associated with successful teams or memorable tournament moments experience heightened demand, aligning with the increased interest in competitive play during these events. The intersection of operations and esports introduces an additional layer of complexity to the market, where strategic investors can leverage the dual impact of these influential factors for larger returns.

A further opportunity that has not been developed to its fullest has been renting items for players to flaunt without paying full price. Similar to subscription models like Netflix and Spotify, the platform Loot Bear offers different plans for players to rent a set number of items from their repertoire. At the same time, investors can rent these items on the marketplace for a fraction of their total value, giving them additional returns. This dynamic between players and investors has not been maximized yet, and it has proven so far to be a useful alternate source of income.

Navigating the dynamic CS:GO skin market during events like the Steam Summer Sale and in-game operations requires a nuanced approach. Investors should remain vigilant, monitor market trends, and anticipate shifts in demand. Recognizing the potential impact of these events on specific skins allows for informed decision-making. For investors seeking short-term gains, the Steam Summer Sale provides an opportune moment to capitalize on the increased trading activity. Tactical buying and selling during this period can yield favorable returns. In contrast, in-game operations offer a longer-term investment landscape. The exclusivity and scarcity of operation-specific skins present a unique value proposition. Investors can strategically position themselves during operations, anticipating the gradual appreciation of these items as they become rarer in the market. The Steam Summer Sale and in-game operations serve as dual engines propelling the CS:GO skin market.

The Summer Sale creates short-term surges in activity and demand, while operations introduce elements of exclusivity and scarcity, shaping the trajectory of skin prices over a more extended period. Understanding and navigating these events empower investors to leverage market dynamics and capitalize on the CS:GO skin economy.

Risks and Regulations

This chapter discusses the various facets of the virtual economy to consider before making an investment, as its lack of regulation has offered opportunities for criminals to profit, and it has also made formalizing a major return and paying taxes complicated.

The Complex Landscape of the Gambling Sub-Market

The evolution of the CS:GO gambling sub-market, particularly the introduction of skin betting on professional matches, has not only reshaped the gaming landscape but has also presented unique opportunities for investors. Betting websites have elevated the stakes by allowing users to wager their skins on the outcomes of professional CS:GO matches, creating an additional layer of excitement that resonates with a broad spectrum of spectators.

Investors keen on navigating the dynamic world of esports and gambling find themselves at the nexus of two burgeoning industries. The rapid expansion of the CS:GO gambling market, while raising ethical concerns, brings forth a landscape ripe with potential financial opportunities. The unregulated nature of these platforms, while a source of concern for fair play and fraudulent activities, offers investors the chance to capitalize on a market that is yet to be fully defined and regulated by authorities.

The lack of oversight has given rise to unique investment prospects, especially for those who can navigate the regulatory challenges that come with the territory. Despite the ethical debates surrounding the convergence of gaming and gambling, some investors see the untapped potential in a market where demand continues to surge. As the industry grapples with the need for clearer ethical guidelines, investors have the opportunity to shape the trajectory of the CS:GO gambling sector by advocating for responsible practices and transparency.

In this dynamic landscape, where the lines between gaming, gambling, and esports intersect, investors can position themselves strategically. The association of CS:GO gambling with popular content creators adds a layer of influence, creating opportunities for partnerships and collaborations that can enhance the visibility and profitability of ventures in the sector. Whether it's supporting initiatives for responsible promotion or investing in platforms that prioritize fair play, investors have the chance to contribute to the maturation of the CS:GO gambling sub-market, adding to its validity and potential. Ultimately, for investors with a keen eye for navigating uncharted territories, the CS:GO gambling sub-market presents a frontier of opportunity. The convergence of gaming and gambling, while accompanied by challenges, also opens doors to innovative ventures, partnerships, and initiatives that can shape the future of this dynamic and evolving sector.

It is important to note the risks that most governments have no formal method to tax gains made from Counter-Strike: Global Offensive investments. Most collectibles are taxed with capital gains, but because of the complicated methods of selling CS:GO skins, it is possible new tax methods may be set in place, partially by its underlying dependency on cryptocurrency and intermediaries to conduct the transactions. It is complicated even for the investor himself to track exact gains, especially if he does trade with other players or on the Steam Community Market, so it's best to keep a log of all transactions, buy/sell orders and trades and discuss with a tax professional.

Illegal Activities

In the ever-changing world of CS:GO skins, where the game's virtual economy collides with real-world investments, there's a dark side that not many discuss. A pertinent issue is underage gambling, which is caused by a current near-zero oversight. This has given rise to unreliable websites posing as resellers and gambling platforms, tricking unsuspecting players, and stealing their items. Even though Valve has been sending cease-and-desist letters to these gambling sites, the bigger issue remains - there's no official government regulation for skin transactions, leaving players and investors alike open to possible scams.

But that's not the only problem. Money laundering has also been facilitated by the CS:GO market. Some criminals are using the market as a way to clean their ill-gotten funds. They buy skins with cryptocurrency, Steam accounts, or PayPal funds gained through stealing, fraud, etc., and then sell them off on third-party sites, effectively laundering the cash. The lack of formal anti-money laundering measures adds to the situation, letting these illegal activities continue without reprimand. Investors should be wary about what is going on and educate themselves on common scams. Players and investors need to be constantly informed, knowing the methods employed by these fraudulent users in the market. This echoes the issue that is addressing underage gambling and imposter websites through a sold legal framework, since it can reduce the risk of these occurrences exponentially.

The lack of official government regulations for skin transactions is like sailing without a compass. Exploring further the economic loss of these activities is necessary to emphasize the need for clear frameworks to keep the market running properly. In this uncertain legal landscape, education is a flashlight in the dark. Players and investors alike need proper guidance to spot potential scams in the CS:GO market. The call for a collective effort, as recommended, is loud and clear. Only when everyone commits to being transparent and establishing a better framework can the CS:GO skin market become a better investment vehicle for entrepreneurs, and a better player experience for gamers.

The Future of the Market

This chapter further develops the notion that the CS:GO Marketplace and the ideas that derive from it have only begun to show, and it resalts the potential the market has to change lives financially.

Careers Made From CS:GO

In the ever-evolving landscape of CS:GO, career trajectories have become as diverse as the game itself. A remarkable journey unfolds when professional players like Jordan "n0thing" Gilbert transition seamlessly into the realm of full-time streamers. N0thing's story is a testament to the malleability of skills acquired in competitive play, where his expertise and charisma find a new canvas on platforms like Twitch and YouTube. His engaging content not only entertains but serves as an educational resource, offering insights into the intricate nuances of playing CS:GO competitively. This shift signifies a departure from conventional esports avenues, proving that a player's prowess extends beyond the tournament stage.

Beyond the players, the world of CS:GO broadcasts has forged alternative career paths, with figures like

Jason "Moses" O'Toole and Anders Blume emerging as prominent commentators and analysts. Their roles go beyond narrating the action; they provide astute insights and dissect complex strategies, earning them iconic status in the CS:GO community. Their careers underscore a growing demand for articulate individuals capable of making esports accessible, bridging the gap between seasoned enthusiasts and newcomers.

The explosive growth of CS:GO has spurred a parallel demand for esports journalism, unearthing narratives that define the players, teams, and tournaments. Duncan "Thorin" Shields stands as a paragon in this field. Through deep-dive analyses, interviews, and thought-provoking content, Thorin has carved a niche as a respected figure in esports journalism. His work peels back the layers of the CS:GO world, offering audiences a richer understanding of the industry's intricacies, challenges, and triumphs.

CS:GO's impact extends beyond content creators to encompass team management and organizational leadership roles. Matthew "Nadeshot" Haag's trajectory from a professional Call of Duty player to the founder of 100 Thieves exemplifies this shift. His journey exemplifies the fusion of astute business acumen with a profound passion for gaming, resulting in entrepreneurial success within the esports realm. Although the team does not currently play CS:GO, Nadeshot's venture into team ownership highlights the multifaceted opportunities flourishing within the professional gaming ecosystem as a whole. This company, among others, have had a ripple effect on the CS:GO Economy, as teams and players playing on the official majors have the opportunity to have stickers available on the open marketplace, giving more opportunities to investors and fanatics.

The world of CS:GO has evolved into a fertile ground, nurturing a variety of careers. From players turned streamers to commentators, journalists, team owners, and game developers, the ecosystem is a testament to its versatility. This adds economic potential, as some public corporations are linked to the game indirectly, such as the Faze eSports company promoting CS:GO as one of its games. The presented case studies emphasize that success isn't confined to the heated moments of competition but thrives in the diverse roles that contribute to the flourishing tapestry of esports. The CS:GO journey is an unfolding narrative where passion, skills, and innovation collide, shaping a dynamic landscape that transcends traditional boundaries.

CS2 Release and Its Profound Impact

The highly anticipated release of Counter-Strike 2 marked a pivotal moment in the game's storied history, ushering in a wave of relevant features that continue to reverberate through the gaming economy. This significant milestone not only overhauled the game's graphics but also introduced transformative changes to match dynamics. The ripple effects of these alterations have been profound, creating a surge in the esports fanbase as novel tactics emerged in competitive matches.

Beyond the realm of gameplay, the comprehensive changes to lighting and imaging have unlocked a realm of possibilities for skin customization. This "facelift" on skins not only enhanced their aesthetic appeal but also granted some previously unpopular skins increased value due to their reflective properties. The update's impact extended beyond the existing player base, attracting new players eager to experience the revamped gaming environment. For investors astute enough to have cultivated their collections before this monumental update, the financial rewards have been substantial.

However, the CS2 release also underscored the significant influence Valve wields over the CS:GO community and the skin market. The dynamics and rules established by the parent corporation can markedly impact the investment landscape, causing a degree of preoccupation among investors who find themselves at the mercy of the gaming company. Fortunately, Valve's recognition of the skin market's profitability has aligned their interests with those of investors. The symbiotic relationship between the gaming community, investors, and Valve fosters optimism for the continued growth of the Counter-Strike: Global Offensive market. As the game evolves, so too does the potential for financial gains and the immersive experience for players, investors, and collectors alike.

Conclusion

In navigating the intricate contours of the Videogame Economy inside Counter-Strike: Global Offensive (CS:GO), we find ourselves immersed in an evolving economic paradigm. Beyond the traditional confines of gaming, CS:GO has emerged as a vibrant economic ecosystem, where digital items hold tangible value, and the virtual marketplace mirrors the dynamics of collectible investments and traditional assets. CS:GO transcends its role as mere entertainment, morphing into a self-sustaining economy with its pulse rooted in digital assets. The advent of skins, initially perceived as cosmetic additions, has proven transformative. Valve's brilliance lies not just in crafting a compelling gameplay experience but in tapping into the psychology of the modern gamer—immersing them in both the competitive thrill and the allure of exclusive digital collectibles. Investors, drawn by the possibility of exponential returns, navigate this uncharted economic territory where virtual assets can have life-changing implications. The secondary market, fueled by an exuberant community of players, collectors, and content creators, stands as a testament to the burgeoning investment potential within the Videogame

Economy. It's an arena where traditional financial paradigms converge with the fortunes of digital collectibles, creating a unique blend of risk and reward.

Yet, amid the prosperity, legal intricacies and regulatory ambiguities cast a shadow. The absence of clear frameworks create illegal and unfortunate opportunities in areas such as underage gambling and money laundering, raising ethical questions. The Videogame Economy, still in its nascent stages, grapples with the need for responsible oversight to ensure the well-being of its diverse participant base. Culture and content creators emerge as influential architects shaping the market's narrative. Influencers, memes, and contemporary sub-culture dynamics, akin to renowned YouTubers discussing the stock market, dictate the fate of certain skins. Publicized predictions and theories influence pricing, ushering in pump-and-dump schemes and novel investment strategies driven by the novel digital zeitgeist. On a global scale, the influence of China and the intersection of cryptocurrency with skins become pivotal considerations. These forces, while distinct, punctuate the interconnectedness of the digital economy with global dynamics. China's sway over the CS:GO market, coupled with the fusion of cryptocurrency, and skins, highlights the far-reaching impact of external factors on the gaming economy.

Exploring the Steam Summer Sale and in-game operations reveals the interplay between market dynamics and player engagement within the CS:GO economy. Surges in skin prices during these events become reflections of the intricate interplay between supply, demand, and the quest for unique virtual assets. These phenomena unveil the dynamic nature of the CS:GO economy, where the flow of market forces mirror the heartbeat of player interaction. Investors must be wary of the risks involved with the market, but they could have an opportunity to make major returns on their investments, all while enjoying their digital assets. The Videogame Economy, with all its complexities and potential, is a realm where pixels not only hold value but also invite participants to redefine the boundaries of digital landscapes. As investors navigate this pixelated frontier and players engage in the ever-evolving landscapes of games, one thing is certain—the journey has just begun.

Videogame Economy Dictionary

The following are important terms to consider when starting an investment journey in CS:GO, or any other videogame, as well as doing research on the topics.

1. Microtransaction: a payment of very small value, especially for a special feature of a product such as a videogame
2. Skin: Skins in Counter-Strike: Global Offensive are weapon finishes that alter the cosmetic look in-game. These are obtained through cases that have a randomized chance of getting a skin from different categories: Industrial Grade (uncommon), Mil-Spec and High Grade (rare), Restricted and Remarkable (Mythical), and Classified and Exotic (Legendary). Skins also vary in condition, making each one unique. Skins can be viewed by others, and have been updated to include player models, gloves, and knives apart from weapons. They are a microtransaction that alter the player experience without being necessary for enjoyment.

3. Case: A "loot box" style item similar to unwrapping a gift with randomized probabilities of unlocking different types of skins, skewed by their respective ranking and quality. They are opened with "keys".

4. eSports: A multiplayer videogame played competitively for spectators to view, in Counter-Strike: Global Offensive, eSports competitions add a layer of "hype" to the value of specific items.

5. Non-Fungible-Token (NFT): A unique digital identifier that certifies the ownership of a digital good. These are commonly used to certify owners of digital art, virtual videogames, and other goods in the internet of things economy.

Recommended Readings

The following are different readings done by me to better understand the different concepts developed in the book. Although I have not directly referenced them in their entirety in the book, they were all essential in the triangulation and dissemination of the topics discussed. For further analysis, I recommend reading them to find new areas of study and/or perspectives.

Aallo, M. (2022). The fascination of virtual skins and consumers buying behaviour in Counter Strike Global Offensive.

Böffel, C., Würger, S., Müsseler, J., & Schlittmeier, S. J. (2022). Character Customization With Cosmetic Microtransactions in Games: Subjective Experience and Objective Performance. *Frontiers in Psychology, 12,* 770139.

Brett Molina, Jon Swartz, Jefferson Graham. It's in the game: The rise of EA Sports microtransactions. *USA Today*. Accessed October 23, 2023.

Burton, B. J., & Jacobsen, J. P. (1999). Measuring returns on investments in collectibles. Journal of Economic Perspectives, 13(4), 193-212.

Courage, A. H. S., Power, A. H. S., Wisdom, A. H. S., & Quests, N. S. Are Microtransactions Bad for the Gaming Subculture?.

Coutinho, T. D. O. S. B. (2021). The Microtransaction Business Model: A Study on Modern Videogame Monetization and the Economic Sustainability of Microtransactions (Doctoral dissertation, ISCTE-Instituto Universitario de Lisboa (Portugal)).

Dalio, R. (2020). *The changing world order: Why nations succeed and fail*. Avid Reader Press.

dos Santos, G. G. C. (2020). *Comparing eSports and Why Do People Watch Them, Counter- Strike Global Offensive Through the Spectator Point of View* (Doctoral dissertation, Universidade da Beira Interior (Portugal)).

GDC (2015). "Building the Content that Drives the Counter-Strike: Global Offensive Economy [Video]. YouTube. https://www.youtube.com/watch?v=gd_QeY9u ATA&t=28s."

Glaser, T. STEAM AND THE PLATFORMIZATION OF VIRTUAL GOODS. *SPIEL FORMEN*, 139.

Hardenstein, T. S. (2017). Skins in the game: Counter-strike, esports, and the shady world of online gambling. *UNLV Gaming LJ*, *7*, 117.

Holden, J. T., & Ehrlich, S. C. (2017). Esports, skins betting, and wire fraud vulnerability. *Gaming Law Review*, *21*(8), 566-574.

Kleine, J., Peschke, T., & Wagner, N. (2020). Rich men's hobby or question of personality: who considers collectibles as alternative investment?. *Finance Research Letters*, *35*, 101307.

Kubera. *Protect your portfolio with Collectible Investments*. Kubera. (n.d.). https://www.kubera.com/blog/collectible-investments

McCaffrey, M. (2019). The macro problem of microtransactions: The self-regulatory challenges of video game loot boxes. Business Horizons, 62(4), 483-495.

Mekacher, A., Bracci, A., Nadini, M., Martino, M., Alessandretti, L., Aiello, L. M., & Baronchelli, A.

(2022). How rarity shapes the NFT market. *arXiv preprint arXiv:2204.10243*, 9.

Nelanthi Hewa The Canadian Press. "Can We Call Video Game Transactions Gambling?" *Toronto Star (Canada)*, 23 June 2018.

Nguyen, P. (2022). *Easy skins, easy life: a chronological case study of loot boxes and transferable cosmetic items in the video game Counter-Strike: Global Offensive* (Doctoral dissertation).

Rhiannon, A., & Varanasi, L. (2022, July 27). *7 types of collectibles that have historically offered bankable returns*. Business Insider. https://www.businessinsider.com/personal-finance/collectible-investments-valuable-types

Rizani, M. N., & Iida, H. (2018, October). Analysis of counter-strike: Global offensive. In *2018 International Conference on Electrical Engineering and Computer Science (ICECOS)* (pp. 373-378). IEEE.

Satchell, S. (Ed.). (2009). *Collectible investments for the high net worth investor*. Academic Press.

Snow, T. D. (2022). *Investing QuickStart Guide-: The Simplified Beginner's Guide to Successfully*

Navigating the Stock Market, Growing Your Wealth & Creating a Secure Financial Future. ClydeBank Media LLC.

Tamir, A. (2020). Commodity Fetishism in Computer Games: In-Game Item Consumptions of Counter Strike: Global Offensive Players. *Sosyal Mucit Academic Review, 1*(1), 45-72.

Tamplin, T. (2023, May 23). *Collectibles investments: Meaning, types, risks, & strategies.* Finance Strategists. https://www.financestrategists.com/wealth-management/alternative-investment/collectibles-investments/#tax-and-legal-considerations-of-collectibles-investments

Taylor, E. (2022). An Investigation on the Pricing of Virtual Items & Digital Commodities: Evidence From the Counter-Strike: Global Offensive Market (Doctoral dissertation, Washington State University).

Walgreen, D. (2010). Investing in Collectibles. *Erasmus University.*

Wang, Q., Li, R., Wang, Q., & Chen, S. (2021). Non-fungible token (NFT): Overview, evaluation, opportunities and challenges. arXiv preprint arXiv:2105.07447.

Yamamoto, Kei'Ichiro, and Victoria McArthur. "Digital economies and trading in counter strike global offensive: How virtual items are valued to real world currencies in an online barter-free market." *2015 IEEE Games Entertainment Media Conference (GEM)*, 2015, https://doi.org/10.1109/gem.2015.7377220.

Zentler, Riordan. "Game On: 'Microtransactions' Are Rampant in the Gaming Industry." *Spokesman-Review, The (Spokane, WA)*, 9 July 2020.

ALEJANDRO GONZÁLEZ-BETANCOURT

THE VIDEOGAME ECONOMY